A BREAKTHROUGH OF A PROPHET

PROPHETESS SOLMARY ALICEA

No part of this book may be reproduced in any form or by any electronic or mechanical means including information storage and retrieval systems, without permission in writing from the author.

2015 © SOLMARY ALICEA

ISBN Number: 978-0692468074

Printed in the United States of America

Scripture quotations taken from the New King James & King James Version. Copyright © 1982 by Thomas Nelson, Inc. Used by permission. All rights reserved.

Cover Art credit:
Works Of His Hands Self-Publishing
Interior book design by:
Works Of His Hands Self-Publishing Consultants

DEDICATION

I first would like to dedicate this work to the most beautiful woman I have ever known my Mom (Marisol Escalante). To my wonderful father (Felix Alicea) who planted a spirit of structure into my life and the drive to go for my dreams. To my brother (Felix Alicea) and my sister (Denisse Maldonado) whom I respect dearly I bless the Lord that all three of us are walking in the way of the Lord and are on one accord in our faith. There are so many to give thanks to by way of this journey as one way or another many people were a part of my life though the good and the bad. I appreciate my pastors (Jose Reyes and Vanessa Reyes). Lastly, I want to acknowledge that I have only just begun and more is yet to come.

TABLE OF CONTENTS

INTRODUCTION 7
BREAKING THE SLAVERY MINDSET 13
STEPS OF BREAKTHROUGH 19
BREAKTHROUGH 25
THE FEAR OF GOD 33
RUN BACK TO THE ALTAR 41
IDENTITY 47
WHAT'S BEHIND YOUR GIANT 53
DUST OFF YOUR ARMOR 57
DREAM (72HRS OF BREAKTHROUGH) 63
ABOUT THE AUTHOR 73

INTRODUCTION

From the womb my mother had already acknowledged she was about to give birth to a prophet. I grew up in a learning environment where there was a deeply rooted structure of teaching through the word of God. From the very beginning I was taught daily how to walk in my calling and to operate with my gift of prophecy that had been graced to me by the working of the Holy Spirit.

Even at an early age I began to experience demonic attacks by the hand of the devil. I soon discovered that these demonic forces weren't attempting to attack me but those who were around me. I had been given access to the rim of the spirit where I was able to see beyond the natural rim. These forces of darkness were seeking a covenant with me that I might be used to initiate greater attacks on their behalf. Like Jesus when He was being tempted by the devil in the wilderness so was I being enticed to use my gift for evil works.

Born a mute I was unable to communicate anything of what I was experiencing. As a four year old I had the communication ability of an eight month old baby. This was a troubling time for me as I wanted to tell but I could not. One of my strongest weapons was that I never showed fear in the face of what I saw in these years. Now that I am older and stronger in the Lord I now acknowledge that they were trying to teach me their ways and in plant the spirit of witchcraft into my life.

As you travel through my account of what I encountered before I reached my breakthrough of deliverance into a life full of power, authority and dominion I want you identify the root of all the demonic turbulence facing you now. I discovered that when your past generations had a hand in witchcraft practices and demonic activations the future generations are made subject to those activities. Just like receiving a natural inheritance of money, houses, cars and land you too receive a spiritual inheritance from your ancestors past, present and future.

My grandparents were inducted as priests of a witchcraft cult and other family members were tarot card readers. They received hundreds of dollars to practice their sorcery and witchcraft abilities. They had made a pack with the devil unawares. These covenants left a door open for the next generation of prophets to be enticed and me to be solicited for induction into the demonic rim. This gave them access to my life and to camouflage themselves as imaginary friends. I blessed the Lord for my mother who recognized the attack of the enemy on my life and begin to stand in the gap through prayer, decreeing, declaring and rebuking the hand of the enemy that was trying to plague my life.

This work is being released to help you identify what is deeply rooted in your family line so that you may rise up with the authority of Jesus Christ that rest of the inside of you and uproot the any and all curses that were implanted in your bloodline to destroy you and your future generations. Someone must take a stand against the enemy why not let it be you.

DECLARATION

Curse of the Pass Generation

Revelation 22:3-6

I declare and decree in the name of Jesus Christ you will rise up by the strength that God place upon you to renounce the attack of the enemy and whip out from the profound of the foundation the roots that are from the pass generation curse. No longer in the name of Jesus will you turn back to the curse that you renounced AMEN!!

Recognize and grab hold what doesn't belong in your life. Toss it out because you are a part of the Body of Christ, you have the authority and victory in Christ Jesus.

BREAKING THE SLAVERY MINDSET

Many may think they're free because they live in America. Don't get me wrong we are free in a way but are slaves to electronic devices that control our mind, time and energy. Many of us have become slaves to a manmade doctrine that is fueled by religion that obligates us to serve while yet still being plagued by generational curses that have us bound. We have been missed diagnosed with medical disorders that get us ensnared in the systems of this world through the rules and laws that are made to counter attack the word of God that can set us free.

The word of God declares that "for he maketh his sun to rise on the evil and on the good, and sendeth rain on the just and on the unjust" Matthew 5:45. Letting us know that God is yet watching over man in all their ways good, evil, wise and ignorant. Jesus love is focus on a man who doesn't believe in God's ways but applauds in the decisions for our nation falling into fear because of the works of our flesh that control us more having us ignorant of who may come and harm us but, we so call trust God, clapping our hands in services on a Sunday morning but arriving late allowing our little ones to run all over but aren't we supposed to have reverence for the things of God, come on living with one another before marriage because you wanted to know the person first before getting married, willing to gamble the little bit you have praying behind the machine, 'God please I need to pay my bills,' the list keeps going on we carry a slavery mindset.

How's your mindset? Many people say and I was one of them, place your feet on the ground and be realistic. How many of us walk scared to speak about God, but is able to teach our future generations to put God's name out of school, learn about sex at an early age, play with electronics when we are supposed to go to worship God at church, killing our future generations but we can't mention that because many people in the government might cause drama so we shut our mouths. You see we are supposed to be the bride of Christ, but we prostitute altars with false praise and false words.

When Moses took out the Israelites from Egypt they carried a slavery mindset Numbers 14:1-27 NIV. They became desperate, their flesh had over powered them by the simple fact they weren't ever free from their own way of thinking. Are you like them, do you carry a slavery mindset? Are you really ready to grab hold of your blessings? You see this is a great example that not all was ready to be free from a life of bondage. Numbers 14:27 says, "How long would this wicked community grumble against me? I have heard the complaints of these grumbling Israelites." you see that's how this nation we are in stand before God. Let me break it down. When they said, where was God when the twin towers were attacked, where is God when my brother or sister was dying or killed, where is God? You need to notice that it's a slavery mindset that bound us and limits our vision to see what God really wants us to see. God's servant messenger Caleb had a made up mind regarding who God was in his life and his spirit was in a place that was pleasing to God that he was allowed to reap his blessings. "But my servant Caleb, because he had another spirit with him, and hath followed me fully, him will I bring into the land whereinto he went; and his seed shall possess it" Numbers14:24. Where there is darkness is where there is a need for the light. We need to be the light in our cities and in this nation. It's time to remove the helmet of slavery in Jesus' mighty name and put on the helmet of Salvation, so we may enter the heavens on the day of judgment knowing you have done a job well done. You don't want to be left in the dessert like the Israelites were unable to stand and receive of the promises of God because of your disbelief. Standing is a sign of strength!

DECLARATION

Break the Slavery Mindset
Colossians 3:1-2

By the blood of Jesus Christ I declare that your thought, your mind is focus all in God. For you are beloved, and live for him. No more attacks with thoughts that are sent from the devil himself. Once again I remind you that you are covered by the Blood of Jesus Christ, like it says in Revelation 12:11 stand in Jesus name.

Don't allow your mindset be your weakness, remind yourself that it is by his Blood and the word of your testimony that you are an overcomer in Jesus name.

STEPS OF BREAKTHROUGH

What's your step of your breakthrough? Nothing is hard for God or what he could do for you. There are choices you need to make to have a deep relationship with Him. Sacrifices you need to make so you may work fully in him. Many people say yes I will, I'm able to put my all for you God and when it's time do they really stand by their word? It's tough to speak out of experience when God wants to mold me in his liking, it scares me. I needed to remove people out of my path. I needed to reflect myself that certain things I was saying and doing was not pleasing in his eyes.

Before allowing God in I made decisions that I knew weren't right, I already had constant thoughts running through my mind of how I was risking my salvation by pleasing my flesh in many different ways beside sex. I felt disgusting before God but I was also scared to let go of the sin that had me bound. I begged God that I would serve him but please allow me do things that pleased me. So I used excuses that God loves me no matter what, that Jesus died for my sins and because he loved me I was free to do what I wanted to do. I was a fool and every day I would try to worship the Lord the burden of my sins kept haunting me and every minute I thought about my salvation it was difficult to think if I step out of my house am I able to stay alive just one more day before God would strike me down. I became anxious, nervous because I knew my salvation was at risk. The enemy hit me hard in my weakness. You see when I say your first enemy is yourself it's the truth the devil knew my weakness. When you are able to confront your weakness and put a stop to it you are closing doors where the enemy can't hit you in your emotions. You need to confront and admit your weak in certain circumstances and close that door by changing that specific area by allowing God in. It hurts and it scars but you must carry your cross and follow him Jesus Christ. What's your step of BREAKTHROUGH, what is it you need to do to be right before God's eyes? It doesn't matter how many times you fall if you get right back up, repent and turn from your wick ways God will forgive you. It doesn't matter how much you bleed and get dirty, but God will heal your wounds and clean you up. Don't you know he's breaking you, rebuilding you, restoring you in his liking not what you want? He won't give you a burden you can't handle but majority times we put the burden on our shoulders because we believe we can handle it. God won't obligate you in anything he's a gentleman. Sometimes we cry or get angry and scream to God why am I passing through this, why am I hurting, why am I struggling? Hello remember when you place yourself in those shoes, remember when certain people try to give you a word of advice, remember he allows signs from different angles, remember when he used to knock at the door and you ignore him, do you remember your decisions. It's hard to take it in sometimes but the most beautiful thing is God loves us. He's able to forgive us and let us see his Glory and Mercy upon our lives, he loves you. He wants to see if you are willing to drop all things that are wrong in your life for him? Be wise in your decisions you make you never know what may happen.

DECLARATION

Steps of Breakthrough
Ezekiel 36:26-30

In the name of Jesus you are no longer bound, chained down in what was holding you down. For you had been broken and rebuild in Jesus name. I declare and decree by the blood of Jesus Christ that you would not return to the old you; you shall be used to win souls for the Kingdom of God.

Focus now on what God has for you and most of all enter into a true relationship with God.

BREAKTHROUGH

As a minister it's hard to realize at times to discuss certain things to any random person because they might try to judge the circumstances without seeking God for wisdom on the matter. Based off what is bring forth to the open many people don't have the proper mindset to understand what you are going through or where you are coming from in the matter. I used to say I'm an open book and I really meant it. Once I started to open up and show myself to family or friends many had their opinions of how I am and few accepted me. Don't allow others to mark you as a target to justify you with their opinions that could block you from moving forward into your blessed place. In the bible Job's story was tragic in the beginning of the book. He had friends that really wanted to help but through their opinions they to a stance against him and falsely accused him of sinning against God. What upset God about Job's two friends is they misrepresented Him completely. They argued with Job from the humanist position based on human experience, human tradition. They were false in their logic and wrong in their conclusions. They believed man must do things to earn God's favor and therefore suffering is a sign of God's displeasure.

While they both correctly asserted sin had to be at the root of Job's problem, Eliphaz believed God was punishing Job for not doing enough good, and Bildad thought Job was just weeping because he wanted His wealth back. On the other hand, justifying himself, Job was condemning God for being unjust.

It's important to remember, that all of Job's friends were wrong in their arguments. It wasn't until Elihu came along we begin to learn of God's true nature. He confirmed the Lord's inability to do wrong or pervert justice, and Elihu said our good works don't help God at all and our sins don't cause Him loss. They only affect us and those around us.

You don't have to be in a position to go through things; you could be where you are right now and have certain friends or family members give you the wrong approach. Many don't know what you are passing through, but the majority of people would say something about it, just as his friends did. Grab hold of anything you may be passing through and those that try to come around you for comfort or trying to guide you, stop them on the spot. The enemy is slick. Some people that would try to come around you have their own problems and issues to confront.

Surround yourself with people that may help you grow spiritually, help you acknowledge the truth of the reason you may be passing through. God wants to break the routine of our mindset of going to others and seek more of his face. No problem is bigger and no circumstances are too hard for God.

Giving birth to a 29 week old baby fighting for his life from meningitis, I became desperate trying to minister and trying to comprehend why I was passing through such a pain. Desperateness had taken over me. I got mad at God and I confronted him with such brokenness. Many were around me but felt empty and alone. As I kept walking every evening to head back to NICU department in the Hospital Doctors were already giving me more horrible news. I couldn't shed a tear, I just felt like a bad dream never finishing. Finally after 3 weeks past of receiving bad news on a Tuesday my son was placed in my arms for me to feed him. I noticed his stomach was getting swollen and was not a stomach that a 4lbs baby should have. I was so excited that he was gaining weight and made it through a deadly process but once again meningitis had plagued him a second time and this time for sure the doctor was in shock. It was very hard on me to receive this report. I had to divide my time between both of my kids, still attend to ministry and taking care of home was such a stressful time of my life. There are many of you that are reading this that are burden down with trials and tribulations wondering why are you having to go through so much. Where is God in it all and why would He allow this to happen to you. I know it may seem like a fiery furnace right now but I want to encourage you by reminding you that "Weeping may endure for a night but joy cometh in the morning" Psalm 30:5. Keep your mouth filled with thanksgiving and a heart full of praise for God promised that many are the afflictions of the righteous but He shall deliver us out of them all Psalm 34:19.

WRITE YOUR OWN DECLARATION

SCRIPTURE:

___
___
___
___
___
___
___
___
___
___
___
___
___
___
___
___
___
___
___
___
___

THE FEAR OF GOD

Called a prophet from my mother's womb was my fear growing up. As long as I could remember I battled the thought of it every day by seeing things and hearing things. There were moments in my life that I was growing to understand but I didn't want to enter into my calling. The unction to speak the oracles of God started to quicken me to speak on behalf of the Lord. Even as I tried to force my mouth to stay shut the Holy Ghost fire of God burned my mouth in such an unexplainable way that I had to speak. I would try reasoning with God to use someone else besides me but it drew me more interested in my calling as I still tried pulling away from it. I've seen my mother and my aunt how they battle demonic spirits daily. I saw demons entering in places and attacking people. I was confused why God would permit me to see these things but He would not allow me to warn them or speak out what I was seeing. Now that I'm older and wiser I understand where God was taking me and telling me. I battle in my home with demonic forces. Things would come to life right before my eyes. I would visualize scratches and marks would appear on my wooden frame of my bunt bed. Many other demonic manifestations would appear to distract me and cause me to fear the call that was on my life.

Battling within myself I fell into confusion of my sexuality. The grace of God preserved me and redirected me into the true understanding of who I was and created to be. I give God all the glory for deliverance from the spirit of fear. My mother made it a priority to come into our rooms at night to pray over us by decreeing and declaring that the generational alliances that were made all the way back to our 5th generation were destroyed. We were taught how to pray the prayers of deliverance whenever there were demonic attacks trying to hit our lives.

Many people now are trying to portray something or someone to please others just to hide that they need help. God is our 911 he's the one that heals, deliver, break you, rebuild you, renew you and restore you. I am reminded of Jonah in the bible. Jonah fled from the Lord when he was told to go to the great city of Nineveh.

> *1 The word of the Lord came to Jonah son of Amittai: 2 "Go to the great city of Nineveh and preach against it, because its wickedness has come up before me."*
> *3 But Jonah ran away from the Lord and headed for Tarshish. He went down to Joppa, where he found a ship bound for that port. After paying the fare, he went aboard and sailed for Tarshish to flee from the Lord.*
> *4 Then the Lord sent a great wind on the sea, and such a violent storm arose that the ship threatened to break up. 5 All the*

sailors were afraid and each cried out to his own god. And they threw the cargo into the sea to lighten the ship.
But Jonah had gone below deck, where he lay down and fell into a deep sleep. 6 The captain went to him and said, "How can you sleep? Get up and call on your god! Maybe he will take notice of us so that we will not perish."
7 Then the sailors said to each other, "Come, let us cast lots to find out who is responsible for this calamity." They cast lots and the lot fell on Jonah. 8 So they asked him, "Tell us, who is responsible for making all this trouble for us? What kind of work do you do? Where do you come from? What is your country? From what people are you?"
9 He answered, "I am a Hebrew and I worship the Lord, the God of heaven, who made the sea and the dry land."
10 This terrified them and they asked, "What have you done?" (They knew he was running away from the Lord, because he had already told them so.)
11 The sea was getting rougher and rougher. So they asked him, "What should

we do to you to make the sea calm down for us?"

12 "Pick me up and throw me into the sea," he replied, "and it will become calm. I know that it is my fault that this great storm has come upon you."

13 Instead, the men did their best to row back to land. But they could not, for the sea grew even wilder than before. 14 Then they cried out to the Lord, "Please, Lord, do not let us die for taking this man's life. Do not hold us accountable for killing an innocent man, for you, Lord, have done as you pleased." 15 Then they took Jonah and threw him overboard, and the raging sea grew calm. 16 At this the men greatly feared the Lord, and they offered a sacrifice to the Lord and made vows to him.

I felt just like Jonah when God would send me to speak life to people who were totally against God especially in my home town that I never wanted to come back to. I refused many times but now I'm right here speaking the word of God. Sometimes you need someone to throw you into the sea even if it hurts. This time of being overboard will cause you to be separated from some people in order to maintain your salvation or even for them to find theirs. Parents it's time to let your children go so they can find their own way you can't calm their storms all the time, sometimes you need to release them so they may learn and grow in God. No matter how the situation may look if you believe your child is called and have a purpose or need to rely fully on God let them go.

Sometimes you need to return where you weren't wanted to deliver others. You need to die to yourselves so the others may gain true salvation. I needed to accept my calling to avoid the blood of another would not fall on my hands due to my rebellion and disobedience. God is looking for an obedient vessel that will fear Him more than we fear the attacks of the enemy. I have learned the consequences of not following His commands. Put your trust in God and Stand.

DECLARATION

The Fear of God
Hebrew 12:28, 29

Father God I thank you for the person who is reading this right now. I declare by your name Jesus Christ that the understanding of the fear of God may be grounded in their life that they may know and practice reverence of your presence Father. May you Lord guide and give this person instruction on how you want them to walk.

Stay focus, God loves you above all things. May you walk with the fear of God. Train yourself to have reverence of his presence in all things. God Bless you mighty men/woman of God.

RUN BACK TO THE ALTAR

What's your understanding of the altar?

> *Leave there thy gift before the altar, and go thy way; first be reconciled to thy brother, and then come and offer thy gift. Matthew 5:24*

The altar is where you may surrender all on the threshing floor in the presence of God.

A threshing floor

> *16 Then he took the five loaves and the two fishes, and looking up to heaven, he blessed them, and brake, and gave to the disciples to set before the multitude.*
> *17 And they did eat, and were all filled: and there was taken up of fragments that remained to them twelve baskets.*
> *18 And it came to pass, as he was alone praying, his disciples were with him: and he asked them, saying, Whom say the people that I am? Luke 9:16-18*

The parable of the wheat

36 Then Jesus sent the multitude away, and went into the house: and his disciples came unto him, saying, Declare unto us the parable of the tares of the field.
37 He answered and said unto them, He that soweth the good seed is the Son of man;
38 The field is the world; the good seed are the children of the kingdom; but the tares are the children of the wicked one;
39 The enemy that sowed them is the devil; the harvest is the end of the world; and the reapers are the angels.
40 As therefore the tares are gathered and burned in the fire; so shall it be in the end of this world.
41 The Son of man shall send forth his angels, and they shall gather out of his kingdom all things that offend, and them which do iniquity;
42 And shall cast them into a furnace of fire: there shall be wailing and gnashing of teeth.
43 Then shall the righteous shine forth as the sun in the kingdom of their Father.

Who hath ears to hear, let him hear.
Matthew 13:36-43

The moment you are able to obtain what God wants you to hear and walk into, you just have to walk in him because God is going to remove the weeds that are hindering you to grow. Go back to the altar knowing what's in store, what God has for you, don't allow anything to hit you where it hurts; let go and let God. Many have lost themselves and trying to fight with their own strength but how you fight is with prayer, allowing God to have total control, in the secret place of His presence. Your relationship with God is another sign you trust Him to be your deliver, provider and keeper. The moment when I'm able to give all my problems, all my faults, all of me while leaving my burdens at the altar, in the hands of God changes would start to happen. It won't happen when you want it to because it's in His timing. You see when Ruth reveals herself, (Ruth 3:6-9) she approaches him with her best not worrying what could happen. She entered like we need to enter to God by giving him the best of who we are as his bride. Where do you stand, are you able to lay everything on the altar entering the threshing floor you're your all not caring what anyone thinks. Give yourself away in this moment and allow God to be your God and you His people and let Him provide for you, protect you, shelter you and keep you in perfect peace.

DECLARATION

Run Back to the Altar
Psalms 43:4

In the name of Jesus I declare they may first establish the altar in their heart so they may be able to surrender and pray your mighty name Lord Jesus. God you are calling people from everywhere to go back to your altar and we would have the knowledge of what the altar means In the name of Jesus.

It's time to go back to the altar to enter in consecration, confession, repentance, surrender, prayer, baptism of the Holy Spirit, healing, and worship. Enjoy as you enter all into God!!

IDENTITY

Putting yourself first is one of the main ways to get When you see yourself in the mirror what do you see exactly beside your physical appearance? Do you know what you are called for? It's time to know your identity!

Place yourself as a blueprint and what can you see or fix. Our blueprint shows us in every corner and plan how we should be built up. We were born with an identity already planned out from our entry into this life. Growing up in this world many have lost their lives, lost their identity, lost who they're really living for. Within this society filled with confusion, wanting to fit in with the crowd that looks so tantalizing we are being misguided and deceived by the enemy at early stages of our lives. I discovered that there were many things in my life that had me paralyzed and stuck in a life of fear. I found myself controlled by the pride of life. I was ashamed of who would see me go into the pantry so I never went. I needed to have things and struggled to maintain a certain lifestyle that supersede my income in order to look good and feel wealthy. Don't get me wrong I grew up in a Christian based home founded by two wonderful parents that taught me the Word of God and I was surrounded by great ministers equipped in deliverance ministry. I created this image of this person that wasn't me really because I wanted to be seen by great people, seen by people of so called high society. When you are trying to live for God the devil throws darts to misguide you and make you lose focus by grabbing hold of your true calling.

I reveal my struggle and need for deliverance because I know that there are many who have been misguided and lost focus by the lust of this world. You must know that we are constantly must lay before the Lord to allow Him to search us and create in us a clean heart. Salvation is a continuous work and we must continue to sanctify ourselves so that our identity continuously reflects Jesus Christ, His walk, His word and His image.

Don't allow yourself to be fooled by the cover of the outer part of the person because you never know if the inside is a blessing for your life. Be still and allow the Holy Spirit to teach you in all things. Stay in the Word of God meditation on God's holy word day and night. Educate yourself to become the man or woman you are supposed to be in God.

> But my God shall supply all your need according to his riches in glory by Christ Jesus. Philippians 4:19
>
> 31 Therefore take no thought, saying, What shall we eat? or, What shall we drink? or, Wherewithal shall we be clothed?
> 32 (For after all these things do the Gentiles seek:) for your heavenly Father knoweth that ye have need of all these things. Matthew 6:31-32

Place yourself in a foundation that is prepared to grow fruitful in God. For his Glory is great and powerful and faithful. Stay humble at all times, for where you walk God is guiding you in Jesus name.

DECLARATION

Identity
1Peter 2:9

My king, my Lord I bring forth this moment that as they accomplishing to see you in them, they would no longer fall in where they came out from in the name of Jesus. For no longer will they walk like who they saw behind the mirror but as you see them. Father God we thank you for living and abiding in us. Let us speak more of you and less of us.

Now no longer will you see your old self, rejoice because the enemy trembles when you walk because he no longer see you but what abides in you

WHAT'S BEHIND YOUR GIANT

When you think you knocked out your giant do you know there are more giants behind the first one? What or who is your giant? As we study the book of 2 Samuel we discover in chapter 21:19-22 that the Israelites continued in battles with the decedents of Goliath for many wars. The seeds of Goliath contended with the Israelites and sought to defeat them in battle.

Are you fully equipped to not only take out your visible enemy but the invisible enemy hiding in the shadows waiting for its time of attack. By the power of the word of God you can get ready, be ready and stay ready. God is so merciful and so good that He allows us grace to get prepared. Putting on the whole armor of God is our preparation.

By putting on your armor, putting on the zeal of God, placing yourself in the hands of God and trusting that He is the one who fights for us is your first line of defense. It's very important to have a set time to have a relationship with God allow him to abide in us every second of our life. You see when you are able to fear not and walk by faith the devil will get mad, yes he will rise up against you but when you share the love of Christ that true agape love that's stepping on the giant's face. Stand and fight! Stand and grab your sword, grab your rock like David did. You see David was offered King Saul's (1 Samuel 17:38-40) but he recognized that another man's armor was a hindrance to him and was not suitable for him to complete his assignment.

It's time for us to stop putting someone else's armor on and dust ourselves off and pick up our own shield and buckler and slay our giants once and for all.

DECLARATION

What's Behind Your Giant
Psalms 44:5

Father God you are our strength and we know you protect us. I declare right now that you may give us wisdom so we may grow wiser in your word Father God so we may know how to stand in the battle field with the enemy. I want to seek you more and defeat the enemy by your might in the name of Jesus Christ.

Keep in mind we are not fighting against each other but in the spiritual realm. I salute you because now you have refreshed yourselves or just found out how to defeat your giant and stay still and wait on God. Trust that He will fight your battle.

DUST OFF YOUR ARMOR

How long have you been in a fight? How long has it taken you to realize that you've been hit left from right? How long are you going to stay put and not utilize the armor of defense the Lord has given you? Sometimes as a believer, going to church, we drop our guard because through our eyes what we see physically we allow ourselves to be misguided or blind to what looks beautiful through our sight. We lose focus of what God really wants to show us and what he prepared for our future path because the devil plays games with us by deceiving us in places we think is right before our eyes. What you do in this earth is going to reflect your future needs.

How dusty is your armor or do you think you might be covered because you have a membership in a local assembly. Take a look at yourself and check what you have on are you 100% you have it well put and clean for war.

Ephesians 6:10-20 gives us a clear understanding of the parts of our armor that needs to in operation in our lives for protection from the effects of warfare from the onslaught of the enemy.

1. truth
2. righteousness
3. salvation
4. the gospel
5. faith

Are you able to put on each one on the right way how God wants it to be equipped in your life?

Ephesians 6:10-20

10 Finally, my brethren, be strong in the Lord, and in the power of his might.
11 Put on the whole armour of God, that ye may be able to stand against the wiles of the devil.

12 For we wrestle not against flesh and blood, but against principalities, against powers, against the rulers of the darkness of this world, against spiritual wickedness in high places.

13 Wherefore take unto you the whole armour of God, that ye may be able to withstand in the evil day, and having done all, to stand.

14 Stand therefore, having your loins girt about with truth, and having on the breastplate of righteousness;

15 And your feet shod with the preparation of the gospel of peace;

16 Above all, taking the shield of faith, wherewith ye shall be able to quench all the fiery darts of the wicked.

17 And take the helmet of salvation, and the sword of the Spirit, which is the word of God:

18 Praying always with all prayer and supplication in the Spirit, and watching thereunto with all perseverance and supplication for all saints;

*19 And for me, that utterance may be given unto me, that I may open my mouth boldly, to make known the mystery of the gospel,
20 For which I am an ambassador in bonds: that therein I may speak boldly, as I ought to speak.*

Put on your armor dust it off for good. Break the routine that our past generations had planted on us, break the chains that are trying to bind us to lose focus that we are overcomer's and more than conquers in Christ Jesus. Wake up and grab hold of the word of God to fight in the battle, stop worrying about what someone else has by trying to covet someone else's gifting and calling. You must humble your heart, walk by faith and trust God by seeking His righteousness. It makes the devil mad when you are confident in whom you are so you must equip yourself and be ready to declare the word of God with boldness and certainty of who you are and whose you are in Jesus name. You might not be where you think you should be in God but you will be right where you should be for Him to deliver you. The word of God says, "Many are the afflictions of the righteous: but the Lord delivereth him out of them all" Psalm 34:19. Hallelujah!

DECLARATION

Dust Off Your Armor
Psalms 18:32-35

Father God I pray that they may not enter the battle unprepared in the name of Jesus. Let this chapter not only be read but they may dust off their armor that belongs to them. Place it on the way instructed in the name of Jesus.

Now that you are able to put on your armor the way God wants and not what man thinks I decree and declare that you may fight the good fight of faith and endure until the end.

DREAM (72HRS OF BREAKTHROUGH)

I was in a church with hundreds of flowers it seemed as if I was preparing a wedding with so many brothers and sisters laughing and rejoicing. In a matter of a second, in a blink of an eye everything and everyone vanished. It became like a foreclosed building. I walked down the street trying to see if the people I knew were there and the house was abandoned also. I kept walking and entered a street that was pitch black and only one street light was on and it was facing the direction of a house where people were coming in and out. I went toward the house and entered. It looked like a crack home with many rooms and one room I was pushed in and the door slammed close. I was pushed down to a seat, I couldn't move an at all my body was stiff like a rock. There were two women with clothing that was sexual looking and their faces were like models as they looked at me and started to smile their smiles turned into a snake and she got on her knees as she licked my leg. Their tongues were like scalpels and my leg bled dramatically. Another demon pulled my hair it felt like my skin was ripping apart from skin to bone. In that very moment a voice that hurt my ear drum with laughter saying this is why you said you deal with the circumstances because you wanted to please your flesh. In that instance a mirror dropped in front of me and I was able to see the person who was talking. I blinked again and it was a girl who I saw sitting in a chair before me and she said help me and the door slammed in front of my face. I kept walking down the hallway and heard a loud weeping of a woman's voice, I walked in the room and there was a women on the floor crying holding a picture frame and a bible placed on top of the table and I grab hold of the bible once I opened it, it was blank pages not even a number on it. Again I heard a sharp voice hit my ear drums and whispered she was so worried about her husband's salvation and that she had lost hers. A door slammed in front of my face. I started to hear grumbling and growling sounds as I looked toward the direction of the sounds their stood two big huge wolves with red eyes and hair like a porcupines. Breathing like a bull I started running as they chased me. I saw an elevator and pressed the button and suddenly it opened and shut. I press the top number to go up but rapidly it started dropping. I was over heating yet the sweat on my body was drying up quickly. The door slammed open and I entered hell. It was body parts and yelling to extreme volumes that my ear drums felt bruised without any bleeding. I saw a young man who I knew that was down there. He was chained up but it was like thorns piercing his skin. His arms and legs were stretched open. Between his legs was a pot filled with lava steam every time the hot steamed raised from the pot it blew in his direction and melted him over and over again. He screamed louder and louder asking God to have mercy. When he saw me and recognized me he screamed out my name and said please tell my parents to stop putting me as their idol because I'm not God.

On the other side across from him was a cage formed as a bird cage and a pulpit with a demon that had on a suit half snake and half tiger skin laughing at people who were dressed up with fine suits tied up against the cage. They were false ministers who blasphemed the word of God and his name. Around them were huge crows poking them and torturing them continuously. Those who have done witch craft or anything against God became the lava that covered the whole ground and they would regenerate and go through the process of melting over again. All around were huge pillars all around and all the way to the top were false gods and one drop to the ground and spotted me from far and his face was as a bull face with horns facing down. And his whole body was as a strong man. He ran toward me and I ran to the elevator and it shut then started to go up little by little but as it was going up in a slow pace it started to fill up with blood until it filled to the top. In that desperate moment trying to find air I heard a clear voice speak while writing on the wall say, "Tell my people I'm around the corner and this blood will fall upon their hands if they don't do what I have called them to do." I woke up on my bed, took a deep breath filled with sweat and started interceding and praying for mercy for my life and for the people of this world.

That's why a breakthrough is needed in many cities, towns and nations because I have seen the bloodshed and the price that we must pay for not seeking a breakthrough into our promise. God is coming soon but are you ready for your change. This dream sparked a transformation in my life. Until the day I take my last breath I will travel the world testifying of what I have seen and preaching deliverance by the power of the Holy Ghost that can break every chain. Are you ready for a breakthrough in Jesus Name? The time is now! Tomorrow might be too late.

WRITE YOUR OWN DECLARATION

SCRIPTURE:

_____
_____
_____
_____
_____
_____
_____
_____
_____
_____
_____
_____
_____
_____
_____
_____
_____

WRITE YOUR OWN DECLARATION

SCRIPTURE:

WRITE YOUR OWN DECLARATION

SCRIPTURE:

_____
_____
_____
_____
_____
_____
_____
_____
_____
_____
_____
_____
_____
_____
_____
_____

WRITE YOUR OWN DECLARATION

SCRIPTURE:

_____
_____
_____
_____
_____
_____
_____
_____
_____
_____
_____
_____
_____
_____
_____
_____
_____
_____

ABOUT THE AUTHOR

Prophetess Solmary Alicea is an intercessor, mother, daughter, sister, aunt and friend. She resides in Cleveland, Ohio with her two beautiful children and family. She fellowships at Iglesia Nueva Vida (New Life) located under the leadership of Dr. Jose and Vanessa Reyes. She devotes most of her time to the kingdom of God and her free time to family and friends.

It is her desire that every one that reads this book would be blessed by the words of her testimony and they will too seek the Lord for their own personal deliverance from the hand of wickedness that plagues us from past generations.

www.ingramcontent.com/pod-product-compliance
Lightning Source LLC
Chambersburg PA
CBHW070950180426
43194CB00041B/2017